# THE LITTLE BOOK OF
# ARSENAL

Independent and Unofficial

THIRD EDITION

**EDITED BY**
## NICK CALLOW

CARLTON
BOOKS

First published by Carlton Books 2002
Reprinted 2003, 2004, 2005, 2006, 2007, 2008, 2009, 2010, 2011, 2012
This edition published in 2017
Reprinted in 2018

Carlton Books Limited
20 Mortimer Street
London W1T 3JW

This book is not an officially licensed product of
Arsenal Football Club

A CIP catalogue record for this book is available from the British Library.

ISBN  978 1 78097 964 9

Printed in Dubai

# CONTENTS

# INTRODUCTION

People say that footballers speak with their feet and that is certainly true of those who have played for Arsenal, but as these quotations show, they and many others connected with the Club can utter one or two words worth listening to when necessary. For new fans and life-timers, here are some of the gems from the great and the good who have graced the Highbury Stadium of fond memory or the Club's magnificent new Emirates home, or in certain cases both arenas.

Whether you want to discover the real reason behind Charlie George lying down in the centre circle after scoring his Double-winning goal in 1971, or who prided himself on scoring good own goals, this is the place to find out.

From Herbert Chapman, Bertie Mee and Arsene Wenger to Charlie George, Thierry Henry and Mesut Ozil, literary giants to illustrious fans, and one Club record-breaker to another – for them, and everyone devoted to the Club, there is only one Arsenal Football Club.

# CHAPTER 1

# GOOD
# OLD ARSENAL

**❝**I am going to make
this the greatest Club
in the world. **❞**

**HERBERT CHAPMAN**

*sets the standards in 1925*

**"**It's one–nil to the Arsenal. That's the way we like it.**"**

*Some things never change –* **GEORGE ALLISON**
*in the film* The Arsenal Stadium Mystery

**"**The Club is so superbly run.
They say a swan serenely glides
across the water and underneath it
is paddling like mad. At Arsenal they
don't even have to paddle, they
just glide. **"**

**MALCOLM 'SUPERMAC' MACDONALD**

**"** With a great name like ours only success is good enough. **"**

*Former Arsenal player and manager* **DON HOWE**, *always demanded the highest standards*

**"**Good old Arsenal, we're
proud to say that name,
while we sing this song we'll
win the game.**"**

**ARSENAL SUPPORTERS**

**❝**It's a magnificent Club
and they really do look after the
people that work for them, not just
the players. **❞**

**KENNY SANSOM**

**❝**I vividly remember a nil–nil with Leeds.
It was one of my all-time
favourite matches – only an Arsenal
supporter could say that of a
goalless draw.**❞**

**RAY DAVIES**
*of The Kinks*

**❝**I thought football's greatest honour was to captain England. I was wrong. It was to captain Arsenal today.**❞**

**JOE MERCER**

*addresses a banquet after Arsenal were*
*defeated in the FA Cup Final by Newcastle in 1952*

❝Going to matches at Highbury is like visiting church, it's the stuff of sustenance for the community's infrastructure. I love it on matchdays when the whole area becomes a sea of red. It's a special thing.❞

*1970s US actor, singer and Arsenal fan,* **DAVID SOUL** –
*'Hutch' in the cult cop show* Starsky & Hutch – *gets the Highbury bug*

**"** That's what they teach you at Arsenal. You have to win, wherever you play – home or away, youth team, reserves or first team – you have to win a football match. **"**

**PAUL MERSON**

**❝**Second in the league might be good enough somewhere else, but not at Arsenal.**❞**

**MARTIN KEOWN**

**❝**My aim is simple – to make Arsenal not just the best in the Premiership, but the biggest and best Club in the world. **❞**

**ARSENE WENGER**

*continues Herbert Chapman's theme some 70 years on*

**❝**I've made my decision and I just hope people respect it. I could have earned more money by going abroad, but I felt this was the place to be.**❞**

**SOL CAMPBELL**

*on signing for Arsenal, 2001*

**"**When you see them keeping the manager, wanting to build a 60,000-seat ground, wanting to win things – that's the ambition I have...I believe in the chairman and the board. I believe they will put everything right to make Arsenal one of Europe's biggest clubs. **"**

**PATRICK VIEIRA**

**❝**I enjoy my life in London. I love wearing the Arsenal shirt and I get a very special feeling every time I put it on. It is something in my heart and I hope it is something that will stay with me.**❞**

**THIERRY HENRY**

**❝** Not a lot of people know I wrote the lyrics for the Arsenal club song, 'Good old Arsenal'. We had a competition on ITV for it and none of the entries were any good so I approached their manager, Bertie Mee, and asked him if he would let me have a stab. He did and within a few weeks they were singing it at Wembley on the way to the 1971 Double. **❞**

*Former player, manager and pundit* **JIMMY HILL** *reveals the story behind the song*

CHAPTER 2

# GLORY DAYS

**❝**We are going for the Double.
There is real character in this side
and now we are going to show we
can win League and Cup.**❞**

**FRANK McLINTOCK**

*after the semi-final replay v Stoke*

**❝**I would not normally say this as a family man, but I am going to ask you for the sake of this football Club, to put your family second for the next month. You have the chance to put your names in the record books for all time.**❞**

**BERTIE MEE**

*to his players in run-in to the Double*

**"** My thoughts turned straight to the Cup Final and I was worried the crowd might injure our players. Some wanted their boots, which of course they had to wear on Saturday. **"**

**DON HOWE**

*plays down the celebrations – there was still the Cup to be won*

**"** I was like an empty shell after
giving everything on Monday
night and was so whacked that it was
almost as if it was someone else
lifting the FA Cup. **"**

**FRANK McLINTOCK**

**❝**Above all we were blessed with a backbone of men with character who demanded excellence from others.**❞**

**DON HOWE**

*in 1971*

**❝**That was the longest three minutes
I have ever known. As Tottenham came
back I remember thinking that perhaps
it might have been better had my
header not gone in. **❞**

**RAY KENNEDY** *reflects on his title-clinching goal in the 1970–71*
*Double season – a scoreless draw would also have been enough to*
*secure the Championship for the Gunners*

**❝**The perfect end to a
perfect campaign. **❞**

*Comment in the* **DAILY MAIL**
*after Arsenal complete the Double on 8 May 2002*

**"** There's a minute left on the clock, Brady for Arsenal...right across, Sunderland...It's there, I do not believe it, I swear I do not believe it! **"**

**PETER JONES**

*commentates as Arsenal score the winner in*
*the 1979 FA Cup Final against Man United*

**“** One–nil in the Bernabeu **”**

*February 2006 and Arsenal are the first English Club to win at Real Madrid, leading to another take on the terrace classic sung by* **ARSENAL SUPPORTERS** *at half-time at Paris St Germain en route to the 1994 Cup-Winners' Cup Final*

**❝**Once we went a goal in front I knew we had a chance because our strength is keeping clean sheets. We had a team of heroes tonight and none more so than Alan Smith.**❞**

**GEORGE GRAHAM**

*after 1994 Cup Winners' Cup Final win over Parma*

**❝**I get a shiver when I think about the Double every now and then, but my philosophy is simple. What is past is gone. What is important is what lies ahead.**❞**

*1998 Double winning captain* **TONY ADAMS**

# "ARSENAL WIN THE WORLD CUP"

**DAILY MIRROR**

*headline salutes Arsenal's (France's) 1998 World Cup win*

**ɭɭ**It sticks in the craw because nobody likes The Arsenal, but you simply can't help but enjoy watching the football they play. **ɭɭ**

**BRIAN CLOUGH**
*after seeing Arsenal equal his Nottingham Forest side's record of 42 games unbeaten, 2004*

**❝**I just think it's something amazing, if you look at the number of goals we scored in these 43 games, and the number of victories we had, and the quality of our football, in modern football it is something amazing.**❞**

**ARSENE WENGER**

*on breaking Nottingham Forest's unbeaten league record, August 2004*

**❝**We worked very hard for each other, maybe some will say we did not deserve to win but our spirit was fantastic.**❞**

**PATRICK VIEIRA**

*scored the 2005 FA Cup Final penalty shoot-out*
*winner with his last kick as an Arsenal player*

**"**Barcelona can make other teams look ordinary but, I'm sorry, [on Wednesday] they looked really ordinary and especially considering we had ten men. But I think we showed against the best team in Europe that we can play good football, even with ten.**"**

**THIERRY HENRY**

*following the Champions League Final in Paris, May 2006*

# CHAPTER 3

# HEROES OF THE SHIRT

**"** The first man in a tackle never
gets hurt. **"**

**WILF COPPING**

*1930s League-winning defender*

**In my time players had short hair, wore long shorts and played in hob-nail boots. Now they have long hair, short shorts and play in slippers.**

**JACK CRAYSTON**

*Arsenal and England right-half from the 1930s*

**"** Coupled with his sincerity and his loyalty to all his bosses, he had a trait few of us are blessed with – an ice-cold temperament. **"**

**TOM WHITTAKER**

*on Cliff Bastin, previous holder of Arsenal's goal-scoring record*

**❝** The Third Division footballer may not be a soccer artist, but when it comes to the heavy tackle, he ranks with the best. **❞**

**CLIFF BASTIN**

*following Walsall's shock 2–0 win over Arsenal in 1933*

**"**To be mentioned in the same breath as Ted Drake and Cliff Bastin is a great honour.**"**

**IAN WRIGHT**

*becomes Arsenal's record goalscorer*

**❝** The centre-forward's drunk,
Mr Allison. **❞**

**TED DRAKE**

*to manager George Allison after he had just downed a*
*bottle of lemonade that was being used to highlight tactics*

**❝**I put everything into every game I played for Arsenal. As captain, I was motivating the side throughout every 90 minutes in front of 50,000-plus crowds every time we played. **❞**

**FRANK McLINTOCK**

**"**They talk about Bobby Moore and Dave Mackay as great captains, but for my money McLintock is more inspiring than either of them. I am beginning to feel obsolete in the dressing room. **"**

**DON HOWE**

**"**When you grow up with a Club and
you end up playing for them and
winning things, you are from that Club.
I was produced here. I was
formulated here.**"**

**LIAM BRADY**

❝There was a time when I had no football boots as my mum didn't have money to buy a pair. She asked for a grant from the town's mayor and one night a delivery van stopped at my doorstep with some brand new boots for me.❞

**ALEXIS SANCHEZ**

**"**The bloke who owned the Wimpy bar at Finsbury Park, where we all used to go on a Friday morning, said, 'I'll give fifty quid to anyone who gets a hat-trick.' And bosh, straight away – he was a bit sick. I didn't keep it all, Ian Ure made me split it.**"**

**JOHN RADFORD**

*recalls a hat-trick in four minutes against Bolton in the FA Cup*

**"**George Graham was telling Lee Chapman that if footballers looked after themselves there was no reason they could not play until 35. Then he looked over to me and said, 'Well, maybe not you, Quinny.'**"**

**NIALL QUINN**

*recalls a much earlier conversation with his old Arsenal boss having broken the Republic of Ireland scoring record at the age of... 35!*

**"**When I am asked why I stayed so long the answer is simple, I never wanted to be anywhere else. I could have earned a lot more by moving, but that wouldn't compensate for all the good years with a great club. **"**

**DAVID O'LEARY**

*on what drove him to break George Armstrong's*
*Arsenal appearance record*

**❝**I made Tony Adams one of the youngest captains in Arsenal's history and I never had any doubts about him doing the job. The modern game is short of dominant personalities, so Tony stands out like a beacon. **❞**

**GEORGE GRAHAM**

**"** As far as I'm concerned, Tony [Adams] is like the Empire State Building. **"**

**IAN WRIGHT**

**"**I knew before I came to Arsenal what kind of players were here. And of course, in training, you can see how many good players are here.**"**

**MESUT OZIL**

**66** When I first came to Arsenal I realised the back four were all university graduates in the art of defending. And as for Tony Adams, I consider him to be a professor of defence. **99**

**ARSENE WENGER**

**❝**He is a truly magnificent 'keeper.
I am lucky to play in front of him every week.
You look over your shoulder and feel safe.
When I started playing for Arsenal I thought
that if the ball went past me it would be a
goal. I still go out with that attitude but
with David behind me I know I don't
have to sell myself. **❞**

**TONY ADAMS**
*on David Seaman*

**"**It doesn't really matter if it's
a back four or a back five.
The most important thing is
that all of us have the same attitude
to defending, which is an absolute
determination to keep a
clean sheet. **"**

**MARTIN KEOWN**

**"** What's it like being in
Bethlehem, the place where
Christmas began?
I suppose it's like seeing
Ian Wright at Arsenal. **"**

**BRUCE RIOCH**

**"**The English players can do a lot for the French guys when they come. We can let them know what they're in for. **"**

**LEE DIXON**

**ℭℭI play to create history and enjoy myself and give pleasure to the fans. 🮲🮲**

**OLIVIER GIROUD**

**❝I think I lost my barnet [hair]
flicking the ball on for all them years
at the near post from Brian
Marwood's corners.❞**

**STEVE BOULD**

*on Arsenal's prolific corner routine*

**❝**I want to get ten [goals] so I can get a coffee machine for Christmas from my wife! She said: 'If you get ten goals before Christmas. I'll buy you this coffee machine.'**❞**

**THEO WALCOTT**

**❝**I think without a doubt that Dennis Bergkamp is the greatest player to have played for Arsenal in the last 30 years, for as long as I can remember. **❞**

**LIAM BRADY**

**"** I've trained against the likes of Dennis Bergkamp and that can make you quite nervous. **"**

*Young 'keeper* **GRAHAM STACK**
*reveals how even in training Dennis Bergkamp is to be feared*

**"** When I first heard the fans chanting, I thought they were booing me. But I soon understood what they were saying and that they like me. **"**

**KANU** *(uuuuuuuu)*

**"It sounds ridiculous, but I always put my watch into the right pocket of my trousers. If anybody wants to nick it, they'll know where to look now I suppose."**

*Superstitious* **STEVE BOULD**

**"**To me, he will always be the
Romford Pele**"**

*Ray Parlour finds an admirer in* **MARC OVERMARS**

**"**Ray is without doubt the funniest player I've ever trained with. It's so important to have players such as Ray involved with the group, for his contribution on the field and spirit off it. I only wish I could understand more of what he says.**"**

**GILLES GRIMANDI**
*on Ray Parlour*

**"**All Europe thought Overmars
was dead because of his damaged
knee. But in every important game
we have had this season, he
has scored. He has got great
mental strength. He is a
world-class player.**"**

**ARSENE WENGER**

*after the 1998 FA Cup Final*

74

**"**Seriously, I was the only player at Ajax who used to have fried eggs for breakfast everyday. It's one of my superstitions. If I don't have a fried breakfast in the morning, I won't play or train well. **"**

**MARC OVERMARS'**

*secret to scoring the Double-winning FA Cup Final goal in 1998*

**"**Those that say it is the taking part and not the winning that is important are, for me, wrong. It is the other way round.**"**

**TONY ADAMS**

**❝If you selected a team of nice people, Dave Rocastle would be captain.❞**

**DAVID O'LEARY**

*on the death of David Rocastle, March 2001*

**❝**It is not so enjoyable to
score goals if the team
does not win. **❞**

**FREDDIE LJUNGBERG**

**"** We've had a lot of good times, but you don't know how good they are until you have the bad ones. **"**

**TONY ADAMS**

> **"**Kanu is Kanu. He is the man. He has the ability to do special things and I love to watch him play.**"**

**THIERRY HENRY**

**❝**It sounds great to hear 'Thierry Henry, record goalscorer for Arsenal'. Wrighty was a great player and will always be a legend at Arsenal. To beat his record is tremendous.**❞**

**THIERRY HENRY**

*scores his 185th and 186th Arsenal goals in his 303rd appearance, in Prague, to become Arsenal's record goalscorer and beat Ian Wright's Club record, October 2005*

81

**"**We play a bit of FIFA together, so it was just a case of a simple X and square to each other.**"**

**THEO WALCOTT**

*after setting up Cesc Fabregas in the 3–1 victory over champions Chelsea*

**❝** We do not buy superstars, we make them. **❞**

**ARSENE WENGER**

**❝**When I was younger, even though I had an older brother, my parents would give me the house key every day. It's in my head that I'm a leader.**❞**

**GRANIT XHAKA**

**"** Maybe I will do that with Arsenal because I like this Club. It is a big Club and maybe we can do a tattoo. We can speak about this in the next three or four years. **"**

**LUKAS PODOLSKI**

*considers getting his love for his new Club in ink*

# CHAPTER 4

# BEAT YOUR NEIGHBOURS

**❝**Arsenal have got as much chance of being handed the title by Spurs as I have of being given the Crown Jewels. They are the last people we want winning the Championship. Now we mean to round off our season by beating Arsenal.**❞**

*Tottenham captain* **ALAN MULLERY**
*sets himself up for a fall in 1971*

**"**There was no way we were going to be beaten.**"**

**BERTIE MEE**

*on the same game*

**❝**It was only 2–1, but the score does not reflect the total dominance we had over them. Even Spurs fans were saying afterwards that they couldn't believe it was only 2–1.**❞**

**BOB WILSON**

*reflects on the 2001 FA Cup semi-final win*

**❝**I didn't score as many as I hoped, but it was nice that I always seemed to score against Tottenham.**❞**

**CHARLIE NICHOLAS**

**"**Jack [Wilshere] arrived here at the age of nine years old and that means that this game is in his heart and brain for the whole season, every year. From the youth teams up, the rivalry exists. **"**

**ARSENE WENGER**

*expounds upon the significance of the north London derby*

**❝**I've not had to tell people like Robert Pires, Thierry Henry and Sylvain Wiltord about the FA Cup because they saw with their own eyes how much it meant when we played Tottenham in the semi-final at Old Trafford.**❞**

**PATRICK VIEIRA**

**"** Even though we didn't win the game people will remember that we won the title at White Hart Lane. That was really important for the supporters. You don't win the title every day. It happened that it was at Tottenham and that's special, but we would have done it [celebrate on the pitch] everywhere. We know it's special for the fans so you can't just leave and go home. They deserved it. **"**

**THIERRY HENRY**

*explains why the post-match celebrations at Tottenham went on,*
*and on, and on and on and on and on and on, 2004*

**"** At the end of the season if Spurs finish above Arsenal I will give £3,000 to charity and if Arsenal finish above Spurs every Spurs fan that follows me must send me a pound which I will send to charity. **"**

**JACK WILSHIRE**

*makes a promise in November 2011. Arsenal finish the season one point and one place ahead of Spurs*

# CHAPTER 5

# TRANSFER TALK

**"**It was a tragedy of monumental proportions for the Club.**"**

*Manager* **TERRY NEILL**

*after Liam Brady joins Juventus*

**❝**I think they thought I had gone past my best, so I had to leave.**❞**

**PAT JENNINGS**

*leaves Tottenham and still has four cup finals in him*

**"A move like this only happens once in a lifetime."**

**CLIVE ALLEN**

*signs for Arsenal from QPR for £1 million and leaves two months later,
without playing a competitive game, to go to Crystal Palace*

**❝** Other clubs never came into my thoughts once I knew Arsenal wanted to sign me. **❞**

**DENNIS BERGKAMP**

**"**If Ryan Giggs is
worth £20 million, Bergkamp is
worth £100 million. **"**

**MARCO VAN BASTEN**

**❝**Tottenham tried to sign me but I held off and came to Arsenal because Arsene Wenger was here. **❞**

**EMMANUEL PETIT**

**❝**Petit borrowed cash from Alan Sugar
to take a cab to Highbury and
sign for Arsenal. **❞**

**EVENING STANDARD**
*the London newspaper relates the story of Petit's route
to Highbury under the headline, It Gets Even Better*

**❝**I am not worried about Premiership football, I came here fully aware that English football is very physical and full of tackling. It is a style of play that will suit me just fine. **❞**

**PATRICK VIEIRA**

*sends out a warning on the day he signs for Arsenal*

**"**Patrick Vieira is simply the king
of midfield players in the English game.
Not one player can get
near him. **"**

**MICHAEL THOMAS**

*likes Patrick Vieira too*

**❝**I've made my decision and I just hope
people respect it. I could have
earned more money by going
abroad, but I felt this was
the place to be. **❞**

**SOL CAMPBELL**

*on signing for Arsenal, 2001*

**"** We nearly didn't sign him because the letters did not fit on his shirt. **"**

**DAVID DEIN**

*on the signing of Giovanni van Bronckhorst*

**❝**I want to explode with Arsenal.
There are trophies to win and
unless there is a change of heart
from the Club, I want to
win some. **❞**

**SYLVAIN WILTORD**

**❝**Despite the global warming,
England is still not warm enough
for him. **❞**

**ARSENE WENGER**

*on why Jose Antonio Reyes wanted to leave Arsenal
and return to Spain, July 2007*

**"**I feel so proud.
Arsenal is a fantastic Club,
and as a child I watched
them play.**"**

*Arsenal 2012 captain* **THOMAS VERMAELEN**
*on signing for Arsenal*

**"**Santi is coming to town!**"**

**DAILY MAIL**

*newspaper headline when Santi Cazorla signed for Arsenal.*

**"**I'm a strong believer in stability and I believe when you have a core of British players, it's always easier to keep them together and that's what we'll try to achieve going forward. **"**

**ARSENE WENGER** *expresses his delight and reasoning behind signing British quintet Jack Wilshere, Alex Oxlade-Chamberlain, Kieran Gibbs, Carl Jenkinson and Aaron Ramsey on new long-term contracts, December 2012*

# CHAPTER 6

# GAFFER TAKES

**❝**There are two kinds of visionary: those that dream of a whole new world, and those who dream of just one thing. Herbert Chapman's vision was of the greatest football team in the world. His genius was actually creating something close to that. **❞**

**BERNARD JOY**

**"**It works. I am just waiting until everybody has copied it, then I shall come up with something new.**"**

**HERBERT CHAPMAN**

*explains his famous 'WM' formation*

**If** I've got a good goalkeeper
and a good stopper centre-half,
all I need is the two best wingers
and the best centre-forward there is.
It doesn't matter what the rest
are like. **"**

**HERBERT CHAPMAN**

**"** Herbert Chapman worked himself to death for the Club and if it is to be my fate I am happy to accept it. **"**

**TOM WHITTAKER**

*as he takes over as manager*

GAFFER TAKES

**"** A wise, shrewd, hard little man...
full of character and pride.
No one's fool, a man-manager
of top class. **"**

*Chairman* **DENIS HILL-WOOD**
*praises Bertie Mee*

GAFFER TAKES

**"** Only the players are important.
I am not important. **"**

*A modest* **BERTIE MEE**

*at the time of the 1971 Double*

**❝**It was a surprise, but a very pleasant one. I had not planned to become a football club manager.**❞**

*Arsenal physio* **BERTIE MEE**
*is appointed Arsenal manager*

**"** He is a hybrid. He is highly intelligent – he speaks five or six languages. He is cool, calm and collected, a great tactician. He also knows a lot about medicine. It's very rare that you find all that in a manager. **"**

**DAVID DEIN**

*continues to make his point about Arsene Wenger*

**"** Arsene who? **"**

**TOM WILLIAMS**

*a lifelong supporter, reacts to Arsene Wenger's*
*arrival on the back page of the* Daily Express

**❝**When he arrived, it was
Arsene who? But I had seen
this guy at close quarters.
I had seen him work at Monaco,
seen how he dealt with players
and the public in general. **❞**

**DAVID DEIN**

*sets the fans straight*

**ff** He took time to understand me, to understand my wild side. He worked on my psychology. He spent many hours talking to me and he understood what I could and could not do. When I think about what I could have become, I owe everything I am now down to Arsene. He is the greatest man I know. **JJ**

**EMMANUEL PETIT**

*gets some help from Arsene Wenger*

**"** It is new to me to have someone checking your diet and giving you all kinds of tips – what to eat, when to eat, how to chew, when to eat chicken, when to eat fish, when to eat meat. You would think that is easy. **"**

**GIOVANNI VAN BRONCKHORST**

**"**The boss screamed. He said we didn't deserve to wear the Arsenal shirt and he was right because we really weren't good, we weren't up for it. But that gave us a boost and the second half was one of the best second halves we have played this season. **"**

**CESC FABREGAS**

*after Arsenal come from behind to beat Liverpool 2–1 at Anfield*

**❝**I think it is very difficult to encapsulate in any succinct way what Arsene Wenger has done for this Club. His discipline and his vision are why we are in a new stadium and why we are redefining the way the game can be played. He has created a young squad that has a tremendous future without having the resources that some other teams have.**❞**

*Arsenal chief executive* **IVAN GAZIDIS**

*March 2010*

**"**He's like our dad in the team –
he is our dad. Every time when we
get a little bit down, he always calls
us to try and speak with us and
that's very important for us and I
am very, very happy to get him
as our manager.**"**

**EMMANUEL EBOUE**

*on Le Boss, post-match August 2009*

**"** Champions continue to go when normal human beings stop and that is what we want to show. **"**

**ARSENE WENGER**

*on what it takes to become champions, December 2009*

131

# CHAPTER 7

# MAGIC MOMENTS

**"**People say why did I lie on the floor after the goal, they said I was tired. But I think I was a lot cleverer than people thought.**"**

**CHARLIE GEORGE**

*reveals it was all a time-wasting*
*plan after scoring the Double winning goal*

**❝** This is a dream that everyone has as a kid to win a trophy like this in a stadium like this for a club like this, with all these players. I have no words, I'm just so happy. **❞**

**HECTOR BELLERIN**

*after winning the 2015 FA Cup*

**"**I have dreamt about this day for many years as a young kid coming through and it hasn't quite sunk in yet. **"**

**AARON RAMSEY**

*on scoring the extra-time winner in the 2014 FA Cup final*

**“**Kenny Dalglish came on at the same time as me and everyone expected him to win it for Liverpool. But here I was, a ginger-haired nobody, setting up the winning goal for Arsenal.**”**

**PERRY GROVES**

*on the 1987 League Cup Final win over Liverpool*

**"**All that was on my mind was Bruce Grobbelaar. I didn't think about what rested on that one shot.**"**

**MICHAEL THOMAS**

*1989*

**"**We won the league on Merseyside,
We won the league on the Mersey,
We won the league on Merseyside. **"**

**ARSENAL SUPPORTERS**

*reflect on the achievement of 1989*

**"**Arsenal come streaming forward now in surely what will be their last attack…A good ball by Dixon, finding Smith…For Thomas charging through the midfield…Thomas…It's up for grabs now… Thomas…Right at the end…An unbelievable climax to the league season, well into injury time…The Liverpool players are down, abject…Aldridge is down,

Barnes is down, Dalglish just
stands there, Nicol's on his knees,
McMahon's on his knees…Suddenly
it was Michael Thomas bursting
through, the bounce fell his way, he
clipped it wide of Grobbelaar and we
have the most dramatic finish maybe in
the history of the Football League. **"**

Commentary by **BRIAN MOORE**

*26 May 1989, as Michael Thomas scores to clinch the Championship, at Anfield*

**❝** That will always be a memory for
everyone else I suppose. The winner's
medal and scoring the goal
are my memories. **❞**

**STEVE MORROW**

*reflects on being dropped by Tony Adams and breaking his
collar bone after the 1993 League Cup Final replay*

**"**I never thought of taking him off.
It's nothing to worry about, it gives
the face character. **"**

**GEORGE GRAHAM**

*after Andy Linighan, complete with broken nose, headed in the*
*history-making winner in 1993 FA Cup Final replay*

**"**My first football memory was Charlie George's goal to win the Double in 1971. After that game I decided to become an Arsenal fan.**"**

**PAUL DAVIS**

**❝**I don't even know what I was doing the facials were going crazy! I've seen a couple [of pictures] and it was just euphoria after and I jumped in the crowd. **❞**

**DANNY WELBECK**

*after scoring the winner against champions to be*
*Leicester City in 2016*

**"** My image of the day will always be of the joy of the whole team when he broke the record. That shows how he is accepted by everyone. It was an historical moment. Maybe it will be 100 years before the record goes again. After all, it has stood for so long and Arsenal had some great strikers. **"**

**ARSENE WENGER**
*on Wright's goalscoring record*

146

**"** We won the league in Manchester,
We won the league in Manchester,
We won the league at Old Trafford,
We won the league in Manchester. **"**

**ARSENAL SUPPORTERS**

*reflect on the achievements of 2002*

**❝**There wasn't a lot of support, so I thought, 'Why not?' and next thing I knew it was in the back of the net.**❞**

**RAY PARLOUR**

*explains his opening goal in the FA Cup Final 2002*

**"**I started clapping myself, until I realised that I was Sunderland's manager.**"**

**PETER REID**

*after Dennis Bergkamp scores against Sunderland*

**❝** What a goal that is; one of the great solo goals in Premier League history from Cesc Fabregas. That has set the Emirates alight. Absolutely magnificent. **❞**

**IAN DARKE**

*Sky Sports commentator, after Cesc Fabregas scored Arsenal's second in a 3–0 win against Tottenham, running half the pitch directly from a Spurs kick-off*

**❝**The feeling I had when I scored was amazing. Now I know how people feel when they score for the Club they support. I will always remember tonight. **❞**

**THIERRY HENRY**

*versus Leeds on scoring his 227th goal for Arsenal, in his second spell*

**❝**What would give me more pleasure than scoring four at Anfield? Winning the Premier League or scoring five at Old Trafford. After the Liverpool game my team-mates congratulated me and made a lot of jokes: 'We'll do everything for you tonight! Do you want anything? Just say and we'll bring it running. Can we clean your boots? Or carry your bag?'**❞**

**ANDREY ARSHAVIN**

*after scoring four at Anfield, April 2009*

**❝**Scoring the goal was a special moment for me. This was worth the wait. **❞**

**AARON RAMSEY**

*after scoring the winning goal in a 1–0 victory over Manchester United – his first since his traumatic double leg break against Stoke*

# CHAPTER 8

# ARSENE'S GEMS

**"The star of the season was the squad."**

**ARSENE WENGER**

*at the end of 2001–02*

**❝**I think in England you eat too much sugar and meat and not enough vegetables. It's silly to work hard the whole week and then spoil it by not preparing properly before the game. **❞**

**ARSENE WENGER**

*gets out the broccoli and prepares to change the diets of Arsenal players forever, October 1996*

**"** We all want to be the best and I
believe I can be the best with
Arsenal. I have a long-term
vision for the Club. **"**

**ARSENE WENGER**

**❝** If I don't smile tonight I will never smile. **❞**

**ARSENE WENGER**

*after 5–0 Champions League win over Porto, March 2010*

**"**I used to enjoy movies and going to the theatre, but I don't have much time for that now. My way of relaxing is to watch a football match on television at home. I suppose for most men that might cause trouble at home, but at least I have the excuse that it's my job!**"**

**ARSENE WENGER**

**“**Part of the English game is that it's physical and enjoyable and... everybody I invite from a foreign country who watches the game says exactly the same: 'There's something special here...'**”**

**ARSENE WENGER**

**❝**Every time you feel you have responded with style and quality and to the expectations of the people who come to the stadium, you're happy. You feel you have been a little bit of a help in pushing the Club higher up to a different level. I try to have a positive influence on English football.**❞**

**ARSENE WENGER**

*on reaching 500 games in charge of Arsenal, August 2005*

**❝** I chose a team sport. There is a kind of magic when men unite their energies to express a common idea. That is when sport becomes beautiful. The unhappiness of man comes when he finds himself alone to fight against the problems he must face. **❞**

**ARSENE WENGER**

**❝**I don't want the will to educate to be opposed to the will to win. That makes the educator sound like an idiot. Any manager's approach must be to educate.**❞**

**ARSENE WENGER**

**❝**I think we can go a whole
season unbeaten.**❞**

**ARSENE WENGER**

*makes an outrageous statement at the start of the 2002–03 season*

**❝** Somebody threw me a T-shirt after the trophy was presented which read 'Comical Wenger says we can go the whole season unbeaten'. I was just a season too early! **❞**

**ARSENE WENGER**

*on the outrageous achievement of going an entire season unbeaten, May 2004*

**"**Going back in time, looking back is scary. There's not as much to come as what has already been lived. The only way to fight time is to not look back too much. If you do, it can make you feel anxious and guilty.**"**

**ARSENE WENGER**

**"** My job is to give people who work hard all week something to enjoy on Saturdays and Wednesdays. **"**

**ARSENE WENGER**

*reflects on his first game in charge ahead of his*
*500th at the helm, August 2005*

**"**You do a lot of things in training for fun. It was not meant to be disrespectful to anyone, they just wanted to score the goal and finish the game. Robert came to me after the game, telling me he was sorry and that he had made a big mistake. As a manager, you have to live with these things.**"**

**ARSENE WENGER**

*on THAT bizarre penalty miss against Manchester City when Pires tried to pass a penalty to Henry but failed dismally, October 2005*

169

**"** Aristocrats had their heads cut off in France. I strive to pass on values. Not the right of blood. A civilisation that does not honour its dead or its values is doomed. **"**

**ARSENE WENGER**

*after a famous 4–2 victory over Liverpool; Arsenal trailed 2–1 at half-time having just been dumped out of the FA and European Cups, April 2004*

**170**

**❝** Everyone thinks they have the
prettiest wife at home. **❞**

**ARSENE WENGER**

*after Sir Alex Ferguson claimed his Manchester United side had been
the best team in England despite Arsenal winning the Double in 2002*

# CHAPTER 9

# IT'S GREAT TO BE A GOONER

**"**The fans' passion for their club is just incredible. It's true love. They give everything for Arsenal and, for me, a Frenchman, with a different culture, it's amazing.**"**

**LAURENT KOSCIELNY**

**" Once an Arsenal man, always an Arsenal man. "**

**BOB WILSON**

**"**Everyone knows I'm an Arsenal supporter, I watch them all the time, and for someone like myself who grew up standing on the terraces and then jumped over and played with the players I actually idolised was just fantastic.**"**

**CHARLIE GEORGE**

*on fulfilling his boyhood dreams*

**"**I love the crowd and the atmosphere that you can only get by being around a bunch of Londoners at Arsenal.**"**

**ROGER DALTREY**
*of The WHO*

**"**I have not a single bad word to say for The Arsenal – it is a great Club to play for.**"**

**CHARLIE NICHOLAS**

**"**I was very very lucky to play for Arsenal and win all those trophies, but when people turned up for my testimonial in appreciation for what I had done for the Club, it was very humbling. Very emotional, but it is every time I go back to Highbury, even as a spectator.**"**

**PAUL MERSON**

**❝**I can't wait to put the boots back on and step out in the old red and white of my beloved Arsenal.**❞**

**IAN WRIGHT'S**

*passion is still clear as he prepares for a
Masters Tournament at the age of 37*

**❝**I told my son Josh that Howard Wilkinson wanted Daddy to play for England. He told my daughter Olivia and they had tears in their eyes as they asked me, 'Does that mean you're not going to play for Arsenal any more?'**❞**

**LEE DIXON**

*following a surprise England return*

181

**"**I feel very honoured to play for this club and captain this place. This club is class and once you are here, you never forget it.**"**

**MIKEL ARTETA**

**"**It's great to be back and play in such a fantastic environment. I am going to give everything for every minute that I play.**"**

**SOL CAMPBELL**

*reflects on his first game at the Emirates Stadium*
*for Arsenal – a 5–0 win over Porto*

**"**I supported Chelsea, but my Dad was a big Arsenal fan so I went to Arsenal and I owe my Dad a lot for that.**"**

**PAUL MERSON**

*proves that sometimes you need a little pointer in the right direction*

**❝**I did not have a choice, but I'm so glad I was born an Arsenal supporter. **❞**

**STUART BARNES**

*former England rugby union international*
*and now rugby commentator for Sky TV*

**"Arsenal will be in my blood as well as my heart. I will always, always, always remember you guys. I said I was going to be a Gunner for life and I did not lie because when you are a Gunner you will always be a Gunner. The Club is in my heart and will remain in my heart forever."**

**THIERRY HENRY**

*on leaving Arsenal, June 2007*

**❝**It was great to come back here. It was unbelievable – it was like I still play for Arsenal. They called my name and it was fantastic.**❞**

**EDUARDO**

*after scoring against Arsenal and drawing
a standing ovation from the home fans*

**187**

**❝**I am really happy here and it is one of the best clubs I have ever seen. Everybody treats you like a king. I really appreciate it. I always wanted to play for a big Club like Arsenal.**❞**

**CESC FABREGAS**

*February 2005*

 I am Gooner.

**ANDREY ARSHAVIN**

*tells fans the good news after signing for the Club*

**"**It's amazing to have joined.
My dad has been a season ticket
holder for 40-odd years. He brought
me up as an Arsenal fan.**"**

*Lifelong fan* **CARL JENKINSON**
*on living the dream*

**"**The atmosphere in the stadium is pretty much what I was expecting; the support from the fans is amazing! They chant non-stop, and I felt very honoured that they even sang a little song about me when I arrived.**"**

**OLIVIER GIROUD**

*on settling at Arsenal*

**"**Sometimes there is nothing better in life than being a Gooner.**"**

**KEVIN CAMPBELL**